Guidance

Have I Missed God's Best?

Resources for Changing Lives

A Ministry of
THE CHRISTIAN COUNSELING AND
EDUCATIONAL FOUNDATION
Glenside, Pennsylvania

RCL Ministry Booklets
Susan Lutz, Series Editor

Guidance

Have I Missed
God's Best?

James C. Petty

P&R
PUBLISHING
P.O. BOX 817 • PHILLIPSBURG • NEW JERSEY 08865-0817

© 2003 by James C. Petty

Scripture quotations are from the HOLY BIBLE, NEW
INTERNATIONAL VERSION®. NIV®. Copyright ©
1973, 1978, 1984 by International Bible Society. Used
by permission of Zondervan Publishing House. All
rights reserved.

Italics within Scripture quotations indicate emphasis
added.

Printed in the United States of America

Library of Congress Cataloging-in-Publication Data

Petty, James C., 1944-
    Guidance : have I missed God's best? / James C.
Petty.
        p.   cm. — (Resources for changing lives)
    ISBN-10: 0-87552-694-2 (pbk.)
    ISBN-13: 978- 0-87552-694-2 (pbk.)
    1. Christian life—Reformed authors. 2. Provi-
dence and government of God. 3. God—Will.
I. Title. II. Series.

BV4509.5.P475 2003
231'.5—dc21

                                2003042456

Rick was a talented graphic designer I met some years ago. He worked for a successful advertising agency, but he chafed at the cutthroat competition, the low moral tone and the heavy pressure to produce. He dreamed of beginning his own firm, where he could set his own hours and be more involved in ministry. Yet he also had a wife and three small children. If he failed, everyone would suffer. He might lose his house and savings.

Rick prayed to be shown the plan of God for his life. He asked God whether he should start his own firm or stay put. But as he did, a disturbing thought surfaced in his mind. He was not sure, but he feared he had missed God's plan for his life back in college. He had gone to the Urbana Student Missionary Convention and signed up to pursue missions, but once he got back to school, he was talked out of it. What would have happened if he had used his skills to spread the gospel instead of creating ads? Perhaps he was now so far from God's will for his life that it was pointless to try to get back to it, much less ask God to guide him within his current, "disobedient" plan.

Rick's problems in seeking guidance from God are common among Christians. For many, their understanding of the plan and will of God has never been sharpened by biblical concepts. One of Rick's major problems was confusing two very different uses of the term "the will of God" in the Bible.

In Scripture, the phrase "the will of God" can mean either the *plan* of God or the *commandments* of God. Theologians describe them as the two wills of God. The plan of God is his "decretive will" and the commandments of God are his "preceptive will" (Hodge 1865, 1:405). The *decretive* will of God refers to God's sovereign decrees and the way they direct everything that happens in the world. The *preceptive* will refers to God's precepts and commands and our responsibility as human beings to apply them to our lives. That is the proper focus for seeking guidance from God. Since the Bible uses the phrase "will of God" in both these senses, it is easy to confuse them. That leads to confusion in our search for guidance, which was one of Rick's problems.

The Will of God: His Plan

Scripture often uses the phrase "will of God" to refer to God's plan. God's sovereign plan is referred to in Ephesians 1:5 where Paul says, "He [God] predestined us . . . in accordance with his pleasure and *will*." Every believer in Christ should have the comfort of knowing that he or she was chosen by God before creation to inherit salvation. Paul continues the theme in Ephesians 1:11 where he declares, "In him we were also chosen, having been predestined according to the plan of him who works out everything in conformity *with the purpose of his will.*"

James 4:15 exhorts us not to make plans with a spirit of self-assurance (to go to a city, live, and make money there) but rather to say, *"If it is the Lord's will,* we will live and do this or that." James does not condemn planning; he condemns planning that does not leave room for God's plan. He tells us not to set our heart on our plans because our life is a vapor, here today and gone tomorrow.

In Romans 15:32, Paul asks the Romans to pray "so that *by God's will* I may come to you with joy and together with you be refreshed." Paul recognizes that he can come to the Roman Christians only by the providence and plan of God; that is, if God has already ordained it.

Peter uses the phrase "will of God" in this sense in 1 Peter 3:17. "It is better, *if it is God's will,* to suffer for doing good than for doing evil." Peter is noting that suffering comes through the plan and permission of God; that is, "if it is God's will."

Rick confused the two terms, and his confusion entangled him in what I call the "Plan

B Syndrome." His logic went like this: If God has a fixed, detailed plan for the life of each believer and he wants us to follow that plan, what do we do when we stray from it? Well, we drop down to Plan B and have to take it from there.

Let me illustrate. Every year I agonize over which plan I will choose for the service contract on my ancient oil burner. Plan A, according to our friendly fuel oil dealer, will rid me from all cares. Under that plan they will fix everything but, of course, it costs more. Plan B is more reasonably priced, but only covers common problems. Plan C gives me an annual cleaning but no repairs whatever. If I have some money in the bank, I tend to choose Plan A. If I am short on money, I choose C, and that, of course, is the year that the repairman might just as well camp out at my house.

In the same way, we tend to think that while God has a "best" plan for our life, he also has some other, "cheaper" plans for people who miss the best. We remember certain foolish or sinful decisions we've made and, because of the consequences, see ourselves on a permanent "Plan B" regarding God's will for our lives. Each time we make another bad decision, we drop down a notch to Plan C, Plan D, and—being the sinners that we are—we soon run out of letters in the alphabet. We think of "what could have been" if we hadn't married so-and-so, hadn't gotten pregnant before marriage, had not turned down the job that would have made our career, or had not blown up at our teenage son.

But for those who are in Christ, there is only one plan, Plan A. This plan holds despite all our stupid mistakes and sins. It reveals the wonder of God's shepherding care, the detail of his love through his decreed plan for our lives. It is a truth that is awe-inspiring, deeply comforting, and yet sometimes intimidating for us, God's proud creatures.

One Sovereign Plan

The Bible teaches that (1) God does have one specific plan for your life and (2) the events and choices of your life irresistibly work that plan in every detail. Contrary to Rick's view, one cannot "flunk out" of God's plan. It accounts for all your mistakes, blindness, and sins in advance. These truths are included in the doctrine of God's providence, which helps us think clearly about God's daily involvement with our lives.

The doctrine of providence was brilliantly summarized in 1648 in the Westminster Confession of Faith (a document foundational to the theology of English-speaking Congregational, Reformed, Presbyterian, and many Baptist churches). Chapter 5 is entitled "Of Providence" and begins as follows:

> God the great Creator of all things doth uphold, direct, dispose, and govern all creatures, actions, and things, from the greatest even to the least, by his most wise and holy providence, according to his infallible foreknowledge, and the free and immutable counsel of his own will, to the praise of the glory of his wisdom, power, justice, goodness, and mercy.

This summary statement affirms that God works every detail of life "according to the immutable [unchangeable] counsel of his own will." This has far-reaching implications for Rick as he evaluates his career alternatives. He does not have to climb out of the hole he dug for himself to get back into God's will for his life. His history, and the decisions that created it, were *within* God's redemptive plan for him.

This validates the decision-making he must now do. He is not stuck in some second- or twentieth-best situation. He stands on the platform of the perfect and wise decrees of God's providence. This provides significant hope as we make decisions about our lives.

But before we proceed, we must ask, "Is this doctrine really true?" What about human responsibility and freedom? What about the problems caused by our sin and stupidity? What about the problem of evil in the world? Does that make God the originator of evil? Some key biblical passages help us understand providence's implications for many important areas of our lives.

Circumstances

Does God control all circumstances in all situations? In Matthew 10:29–30, Jesus says that "not one of them [sparrows] will fall to the ground apart from the will of your Father. And even the very hairs of your head are all numbered." Jesus uses this extraordinary level of care and control by God to allay his disciples' fears when facing persecution and testing. Things that seem accidental do not take place without the permission of God. He says, "So don't be afraid; you are worth more than many sparrows" (Matt. 10:31).

Notice the purpose of Jesus' teaching. He did not give it to establish an abstract principle to be applied in any direction we might fancy. He gave it to minister to the fear of loss, death, suffering, and abuse among his people. It clearly establishes God's total control over life, but for a pastoral purpose that must be respected.

Some might ask, "How can I receive comfort from a doctrine that teaches that everything is determined and implies that there is no use to prayer or human effort?" Non-Christians might say, "Why should I accept a view that makes God the cause of evil?" Their mistake is to look at the doctrine as an isolated truth that can turn any way the logic of their minds leads them. The doctrine of God's sovereign control over circumstances is *never* used in Scripture to discourage prayer or human effort but rather the exact reverse. *Because* God can intervene, we should pray and we should work. It is *never* used to establish God's authorship of evil. That is explicitly denied in James 1:13 and many other passages. Satan and mankind's own sin are identified as the causes of evil.

The purposes for which this doctrine is used in Scripture are to induce humility in us (Rom. 9:20), to inspire praise for God's love for sinners (Eph. 1:11), to assure believers of the indestructibility and practicality of God's love (Rom. 8:28), and to warn enemies of the futility of resistance and rebellion (Ps. 2:9–10; Dan. 4:34–35). It highlights the facts that our individuality and circumstances are ordained by God (Ps. 139:13–16). David reflects on the personal value of knowing that God constantly

8

had thoughts of him. He says, "How vast is the sum of them! Were I to count them, they would outnumber the grains of sand (Ps. 139:17–18).

How many of us really believe that God is that aware of our circumstances? David says that we could not even count God's thoughts, much less pay such detailed attention to our own lives. I weep for Christians who conclude that they cannot enjoy this confidence in God's care for fear of implicating him in evil.

We may have had experiences with some who misuse the doctrine of providence. They are like the man who fell down a long flight of stairs one morning. "Fortunately" the stairs were carpeted, and he was able to dust himself off and hobble to the breakfast table. He sat down, looked at his wife and said, "Boy, am I glad that's over." While in a logical (and humorous) sense that response might be appealing, it only diverts attention from this man's duty to figure out what went wrong and take precautions against future mishaps. God did not reveal the reality of his providential care to excuse us from being stewards of our lives.

A beautiful illustration of God's providence is recorded in Genesis 50:20. Up to that point, Genesis tells the story of how Joseph's brothers sold him into slavery, how Joseph was falsely accused of rape and unjustly imprisoned, how he rose to great power in Egypt, and then saved Egypt and his family from starvation. After all this, in Genesis 50:20 Joseph tells his brothers why he will not take revenge on them for their treachery. He says, "You intended to harm me, but God intended it for good to accomplish what is now being done, the saving of many lives." Every action of the brothers, of Joseph, of Pharaoh, and even of the weather that brought the famine, was under God's sovereign control. There is, in short, no circumstance—from the numbering of the hairs of our head to the movements of nations—that does not in every respect work out the plan of God.

If this is true, what about the results of humanity's evil acts? The story of Joseph previews the answer.

Good Men, Evil Men, and Politicians

Is God's plan worked out by the free and responsible actions of men and women, whether good or evil? It is the question evoked by Hitler, Pol Pot, and the thug who assaulted your child. It is the question of Bishop Wilberforce and Martin Luther King Jr., who fought for the rights and dignity of those of African descent.

This is a natural question in view of the Last Judgment, which clearly holds every man, woman, and child accountable for their own actions. John 5:28–29 says,

> Do not be amazed at this, for a time is coming when all who are in their graves will hear his voice and come out—those who have done good will rise to live, and those who have done evil will rise to be condemned.

What is implied by the story of Joseph is specifically taught in Scripture: every act of every individual is according to the unchangeable blueprint of God. The Bible emphasizes the fact that the most "free" of all people (kings and rulers) work the plan of God. Proverbs 21:1 declares, "The king's heart is in the hand of the LORD; He directs it like a watercourse wherever he pleases." (See also Ps. 33:11; Prov. 19:21; Isa. 14:27; 46:9–10.)

God's sovereignty over people's evil acts comes to purest expression in Peter's sermon in Acts 2:23. "This man [Jesus] was handed over to you by God's set purpose and foreknowledge; and you, with the help of wicked men, put him to death by nailing him to the cross." Peter says that even this arch crime of human history was ordained by the set purpose of God. Yet he is bold in laying responsibility for the crime directly on Israel's religious leaders.

You might ask, "Isn't it impossible for God to be in control while humans are the causes of good and evil?" It is evidently not impossible for God. Our minds cannot fathom how God can create responsible creatures who are truly accountable to him, while all their sin is worked out in strict accordance with the plan of God. Life is under control, but of a most sophisticated sort. With our own responsible will, we work the plan of God, though God does not tempt or coerce our will in any way. Although we do not know how God controls all things, it appears that he generally keeps "hands off" the mechanism of our will. Yet we responsibly and freely choose to do everything as he planned it.

I have heard so many believers say, "You can't have it both ways; either humans are fully accountable for their actions or God's plan is in control." We must resist the idea that if we can't understand how God does it, it can't happen. We cannot insist that we must choose either responsibility or divine sovereignty; that we can have one or the other, but not both.

The fact that both are true is the glory of God's wisdom. We should bow and worship, not get carried away with our arrogant musings about what God can and cannot do. We are finite creatures who lack access to the level of thought or existence enjoyed by God. It is the epitome of good sense to trust his revelation of himself. It should lead us to respond with awe as those who know they are accountable, as his image-bearers.

The good acts of men and women are also foreordained. Ephesians 2:10 says, "We are God's workmanship, created in Christ Jesus to do good works, which God prepared in advance for us to do." Yet, at the same time, again and again we are *commanded* to do good works (1 Tim. 6:18; Heb. 10:24). In Philippians 2:12–13, Paul lets us see the two realities functioning together. He says, "Work out your salvation with fear and trembling, for it is God who works in you to will and to act according to his good purpose." Rather than reducing human responsibility for the Christian, this truth amplifies it by linking it to an irresistible power—God working his good purpose in us. From here we look at God's providence at work in our salvation.

God's Providence in Salvation and Judgment

In this area of providence we step onto the holiest of ground, humbled by the wonder and terror of what we read. If we take the classic Scripture passages regarding "predestination" at face value, it is clear that believers are such because they were chosen by God. We chose him because he chose us. Here are some of the verses that teach this:

In love he predestined us to be adopted as his sons through Jesus Christ. (Eph. 1:5)

You did not choose me, but I chose you . . . to go and bear fruit—fruit that will last. (John 15:16)

All that the Father gives me will come to me, and whoever comes to me I will never drive away. . . . And this is the will of him who sent me, that I shall lose none of all that he has given me, but raise them up at the last day. (John 6:37, 39)

Jesus reveals that God gave him a distinct group of people to save, and every single one would actually be saved. He balances his teaching by saying that everyone who comes to him desiring salvation will find it. He will turn no one away. It is exclusive and personal, yet open to all. Here again a glorious paradox is created by the multi-leveled and mysterious way God governs his creatures. He has an eternal, unchangeable plan, yet God can create a world with true responsibility and dignity.

The way in which God plans and completes salvation for his chosen ones is captured in Romans 8:28–30:

And we know that in all things God works for the good of those who love him, who have been called according to his purpose. For those God foreknew he also predestined to be conformed to the likeness of his Son, that he might be the firstborn among many brothers. And those he predestined, he also called; those he called, he also justified; those he justified, he also glorified.

Everyone who is foreknown is predestined, and everyone predestined ends up glorified. No one falls out of the system. Even those who never repent and are judged for their hatred of God do so according to the plan of God, set down prior to creation. Romans 9:11–13, speaking of Jacob and Esau, says, "Yet, before the twins were born or had done anything good or bad—in order that God's purpose in election might stand: . . . she was told, 'The older will serve the younger'. . . . Jacob I loved, but Esau I hated." The purpose for revealing this truth is in verse 16: "It does not, therefore, depend on man's desire or effort, but on God's mercy."

Paul is not revealing a philosophical capstone that creative minds can use in any way they want. He is showing us the utter extent to which our salvation is by grace alone, originating in the pure and personal love of God for us.

While we may find it difficult to assimilate this strong medicine for human pride, it need not be overwhelming when we use the doctrine *within the pastoral purpose for which it was revealed*. I must say again that theological truths, no matter how biblical, must be used in a biblical way. They are not bullets to shoot in any direction, but only the directions revealed in Scripture.

We cannot, for instance, use God's right to choose as a reason to deny human responsibility or to say that our efforts at witnessing to or praying for unbelievers are meaningless. On the contrary, God's control and predestination is what gives us hope that he will act. It is our reason to pray that God will save them. God can save or justly condemn and he has the authority and power to do either.

Paul mirrors the right attitude towards his unsaved Jewish kinsmen.

> I speak the truth in Christ—I am not lying, my conscience confirms it in the Holy Spirit—I have great sorrow and unceasing anguish in my heart. For I could wish that I myself were cursed and cut off from Christ for the sake of my brothers, those of my own race, the people of Israel. (Rom. 9:1–4)

Paul voices our anguish as we consider the lost condition of people we love. But he responds to this desire for their salvation by fearlessly preaching to his Jewish brethren in every city and praying for them to be saved (Rom. 10:1).

The purpose of God worked out in providence is a huge, unseen reality. If you are in Christ, you can trust yourself to God's eternal, unchangeable will. You are in an invisible harmony with God's plan for your life. There is no Plan B, C, or D. There is only what God ordained by his plan and our accountable actions. In his mysterious sovereignty, both of those become one.

Christ offers that security to anyone who wants it enough to come to him for salvation. It is (to the self-sufficient mind) "too good to be true" that Christ could offer election to anyone who wanted it. He can offer God's chosen, personal love to those who come to him for it. Perhaps the gospel is the one thing in the universe that really is "too good to be true" but is. Again, no one has the faintest idea of how God does this, but he does. We can only gasp at the magnitude and sophistication of his mercy and power.

Toxic Knowledge?

You may be like me during my first months in seminary. I resented the idea that I was not in a position to understand God's governance of good and evil. I said, "How can you believe in the God of the Bible without having this level of knowledge? How do you even know Christianity is true without being able to check this out yourself?" Many have longed to know as God knows. I *demanded* to know.

That was the temptation of Adam and Eve in the Garden (Gen. 3:5). But such knowledge is not given to us *for our own good*. There are several reasons why we would have trouble with such knowledge.

First, God's knowledge is exhaustive. It creates and covers the movement of every atomic particle since the dawn of creation. The plan by which he governs our world is way out of our league in sophistication and quantity of information. God could not describe the ordinary way in which gravity and quantum theory relate and have even one scientist on earth today understand it. Our knowledge even of the processes he has made evident is laughably primitive. Scientists have studied the simplest forms of life for a hundred years, but we have not yet been able to generate even the simplest life form. God's questions to Job about nature (Job 38–42) challenged him to the point that Job insisted that God stop asking them.

We might, however, ask for at least a peek at God's plan for our lives. That leads us to the second reason why we cannot know the plan of God. The information is too toxic for us to handle. Let me explain.

We might, for example, think it would be reassuring to see the list of those chosen by God for eternal life. Obviously, we would want to make sure we were among them . . . or confirm that we missed the list so we could stop trying and relax, eat, drink, and be merry with the time remaining. Knowing with certainty that we would be saved no matter what we did or believed would corrupt us beyond recognition as Christians.

I have also witnessed persons who try to blaspheme the Holy Spirit in order to seal their damnation! Such was their obsession to "know for sure." They schemed that if they blasphemed the Holy Spirit, they could thus control their fate and find relief from uncertainty. They lusted for the certainty of God's knowledge of the future—and were willing to trade their souls for it!

Others might desire to know the day and manner of their death, or the death of their loved ones, or the horrible and wonderful things that lie ahead in life. But the truth is, if we had known what was involved in most of the things we did, we would never have started. We can handle problems on a daily basis, but we could never handle them if we knew them all in advance.

Our knowledge of good and evil is restricted by God's love for us. The good is too good and the evil is too evil. He did not expose the origins of evil to Job, a godly and upright man, nor did he tell Job about the cosmic battle between himself and Satan taking place through Job's sufferings. Similarly, God does not reveal his decretive plans to his creatures—and it is for our good.

The problem of evil has vexed Christians for centuries. Non-Christians blithely brush off the claims of Christ by saying, "If God is so good and also sovereign, then why did he allow evil?" To them it means that either God is not good or not sovereign—or that he is neither. They restrict God's options to the ones they can imagine. Man's knowledge is assumed to be the final, self-justifying, starting point for truth.

It never occurs to them that God is protecting us from information we are not able to handle. One day, I believe we will learn more about Satan's creation and his rebellion against God. We will perhaps learn more about why God chose to save a fallen world, rather than wiping it out and beginning again. There may be levels of irrationality to the origin of evil that cannot be comprehended by finite creatures or that would be paralyzing if we were exposed to them now. We are dependent on the good judgment of the Father who loves us and is determined to give us life despite our rebellion against him.

God has determined that, with some exceptions, the names of the elect and the lost must stay secret until the Judgment Day (Rev. 20:12). The ultimate battle between good and evil, and the reflections of that battle in the providence of God, are best left to God.

Jesus teaches that we are "wired" to handle each day's anxiety each day—no more (Matt. 6:34). With those I counsel, I find that almost all anxiety-related problems are caused by a supposed need to know the future in some form. That is the appeal of astrologers, seers, witches, and all occult religionists, in stark contrast to the man who fears the Lord and counts him equal to the task of governing the universe.

"The knowledge of good and evil," in the limited way we understand it now, was a result of humanity's rebellion against God (Gen. 3:5). Humanity wanted to know and understand the basis for everything God had commanded, but since we are not God, this knowledge created life-threatening problems. There seems to be an experiential component to knowing evil that is lethal. Even what God does reveal seems to be described in metaphorical language that leaves us with questions perhaps God consciously meant, for our own benefit, not to answer.

Moses beautifully states the distinction between the two kinds of knowledge in Deuteronomy 29:29: "The secret things belong to the LORD our God, but the things revealed belong to us and to our children forever, that we may follow all the words of this law."

Moses teaches us to accept not knowing the secret things of God. Instead, he urges us to focus on what God *has* revealed, the words of his law and how we may implement them. He exhorts us not to waste time and energy seeking to unlock the secret plans of God; God wants us to trust him for that. God desires us to focus on ordering our lives by what he has revealed—his Word.

Most occult knowledge centers on finding ways of penetrating the beneficial boundaries God has erected to our knowledge. But Jesus revealed God in a non-lethal, life-giving form. He did not come to unveil the secret things of God's providence, but to reveal how God would redeem the fallen world. He gives us the truth that sets us free. His truth focuses our energy on present obedience and service. God promises to take care of the obstacles in the paths of those who trust him. Jesus promises, "But seek first his kingdom and his righteousness, and all these things [our future needs] will be given to you as well" (Matt. 6:33). We can now return to Rick's situation with these truths in mind.

As Rick struggles to decide whether to go independent, he will not be able to discern the plan of God in advance. He can know, however, that because of the work of Christ, he is not on a permanent Plan B, C, or Z. In Christ there is only one plan: Plan A. He must do the hard work of finding biblical principles and values that apply to his situation. He must gather information on himself and his options. He must pray and then make the decision. Rick can be greatly strengthened to know that he makes his decision in a protected environment. The Great Shepherd of the Sheep, the Almighty God, watches over him. That watch-care is called providence.

The Guardrail of Providence

God's providence is a bit like a guardrail on a mountain highway. One summer I traveled to South America on a missions trip with twelve other college-age musicians. One day we had to travel between two Colombian cities high in the Andes Mountains. We left at six in the morning and traveled until six that evening over a one-lane gravel road. This terrifying road was usually thousands of feet above the valley floor, with hairpin turns and switchbacks every few minutes.

There were no guardrails—*none!* I remember the driver barreling ahead with his horn blasting as we rounded each turn to warn some poor oncoming motorist that we were about to smash into him. Along the road were scores of little memorials to those who had gone over the sides. Because the bus held forty-two and there were sixty-five on board, I was privileged to stand up all day, which helped when carsickness required me to lean over three people to vomit out the window!

At any rate, at one point I was keenly aware that there really *was* a guardrail beside that road. It was the sovereign providence of God. I was comforted by the fact of my invincibility unless God himself gave his approval to our death. I imagined an invisible and impenetrable guardrail, maintained by the living God. (Incidentally, I believe we hit that invisible rail a number of times.)

God's sovereign providence is like that guardrail to our decision making. We are hurtling down the mountain of life with turns constantly confronting us. Yet we can be confident that God has established the boundaries of our lives. He holds us in his hand despite the dangers we face and the foolish decisions we make. Only in heaven will we know how often we bumped into the guardrail of God's plan and were protected for his gracious purpose.

How can we not fall down and worship this sovereign God, who protects us, trains us with his providential care, and loves us enough to teach us to trust him where it would be harmful for us to understand? Shouldn't this create in us an attitude of worship, reverence, gratefulness, and confidence amid a world that seems out of control?

Those who are in Christ know that despite all the decisions we face, the mistakes we make, the sins we repent of, and the things we did not anticipate, God works in all things for the good of transforming us into the image of Christ (Rom. 8:28). That is our foundation as we trust God to guide us in applying his commands to our life and circumstances. If that is your goal in life, you are in very good hands!

Dr. James Petty is the executive director of the Children's Jubilee Fund in Philadelphia, Pennsylvania; a counselor; and a former pastor. This booklet is adapted from his book, Step by Step: Divine Guidance for Ordinary Christians (*Phillipsburg, N.J.: P&R, 1999*).

RCL Ministry Booklets

A.D.D.: Wandering Minds and Wired Bodies, by Edward T. Welch

Anger: Escaping the Maze, by David Powlison

Angry at God? Bring Him Your Doubts and Questions, by Robert D. Jones

Bad Memories: Getting Past Your Past, by Robert D. Jones

Depression: The Way Up When You Are Down, by Edward T. Welch

Domestic Abuse: How to Help, by David Powlison, Paul David Tripp, and Edward T. Welch

Forgiveness: "I Just Can't Forgive Myself!" by Robert D. Jones

God's Love: Better than Unconditional, by David Powlison

Guidance: Have I Missed God's Best? by James C. Petty

Homosexuality: Speaking the Truth in Love, by Edward T. Welch

"Just One More": When Desires Don't Take No for an Answer, by Edward T. Welch

Marriage: Whose Dream? by Paul David Tripp

Motives: "Why Do I Do the Things I Do?" by Edward T. Welch